My Neighborhood

The School

Aaron Carr

www.av2books.com

LET'S READ
AV²
BY WEIGL™
ADDED VALUE • AUDIO VISUAL

AV² provides enriched content that supplements and complements this book. Weigl's AV² books strive to create inspired learning and engage young minds in a total learning experience.

Your AV² Media Enhanced books come alive with...

Audio
Listen to sections of the book read aloud.

Key Words
Study vocabulary, and complete a matching word activity.

Video
Watch informative video clips.

Quizzes
Test your knowledge.

Go to **www.av2books.com,** and enter this book's unique code.

BOOK CODE

P999755

Embedded Weblinks
Gain additional information for research.

Slide Show
View images and captions, and prepare a presentation.

AV² by Weigl brings you media enhanced books that support active learning.

Try This!
Complete activities and hands-on experiments.

... and much, much more!

Published by AV² by Weigl
350 5ᵗʰ Avenue, 59ᵗʰ Floor New York, NY 10118
Website: www.av2books.com   www.weigl.com

Library of Congress Cataloging-in-Publication Data

Carr, Aaron.
 The school / Aaron Carr.
   pages cm. -- (My neighborhood)
 ISBN 978-1-62127-348-6 (hardcover : alk. paper) -- ISBN 978-1-62127-353-0 (softcover : alk. paper)
 1. Schools--Juvenile literature. I. Title.
 LB1513.C377 2013
 371--dc23
                      2013006841

032013
WEP300113

Printed in the United States of America, in North Mankato, Minnesota
1 2 3 4 5 6 7 8 9 17 16 15 14 13

Project Coordinators: Heather Kissock and Megan Cuthbert Design: Mandy Christiansen

Weigl acknowledges Getty Images as the primary image supplier for this title.

The School

CONTENTS

This is my neighborhood.

My school is in
my neighborhood.

I go to school to learn new things.

At school, I see my friends and teachers.

My teacher helps me learn.

I learn how to read, write, and do math.

1
+ 3

My school has many tools to help me learn.

Chalkboards, books, and computers are just a few of the tools I use.

In my classroom I have a desk where I can do my school work.

I also listen to stories and make crafts.

My school has a large gym.

This is where I run and play sports.

I also go to the gym to listen to people from my neighborhood talk.

My parents come to the gym to watch me in plays and concerts.

Sometimes my school has events for the people in my neighborhood.

$4.50

$1.50 per slice

My school holds bake sales, dances, and sports games.

There are many fun things for me to do after school.

I can play on a sports team or join a school club.

See what you have learned about teachers and schools.

Which of these pictures does not show a school?

KEY WORDS

Research has shown that as much as 65 percent of all written material published in English is made up of 300 words. These 300 words cannot be taught using pictures or learned by sounding them out. They must be recognized by sight. This book contains 50 common sight words to help young readers improve their reading fluency and comprehension. This book also teaches young readers several important content words, such as proper nouns. These words are paired with pictures to aid in learning and improve understanding.

Page	Sight Words First Appearance	Page	Content Words First Appearance
4	is, my, this	4	neighborhood
5	in, school	7	friends, teachers
6	go, I, learn, new, things, to	9	math
7	and, at, see	10	tools
8	helps, me	11	chalkboards, computers
9	do, how, read, write	12	classroom, desk
10	has, many	13	crafts, stories
11	a, are, books, few, just, of, the, use	14	gym
12	can, have, where, work	15	sports
13	also, make	17	concerts, parents, plays
14	large	18	events
15	play, run	19	bake sales, dances, sports games
16	from, people, talk	21	club, team
17	come, watch		
18	for, sometimes		
20	after, there		
21	on, or		